DEFEATING MY DEMONS

DEFEATING MY DEMONS

My Mental Breakdown, Through Darkness to the Light

Manda Jones
WITH *Jason Bjorn*

Defeating My Demons © Manda Jones, 2020

ISBN: 978-0-578-65392-1

All rights reserved.

No part of this book may be reproduced in any form or by any electronic or mechanical means, including information storage and retrieval systems, without express written permission from the publisher, except for the use of brief quotations in reviews.

Published by
Manda & Friends LLC
421 Hickory Ave
Eaton, CO 80615

To my wonderful husband and my four children,
all of whom show me unconditional love.

Manda and her four lovely children, 2010

FOREWORD

If someone asked me to describe mental health in one word, I would say conditional. This is because so many factors go into determining each individual's mental health. Personal experience impacts world views and personal relationships, and these elements affect natural resilience. Cultural norms and beliefs, societal stigma, gender, race, ethnicity, socioeconomic status, sexual identity, and access to personal and community support, among other lacking support, have all been shown to have an influence on mental health. Yet, overall, the community is not supportive of mental health treatment.

Mental health services are woefully underfunded, and stigma persists for those who seek treatment. At the same time, the topic of mental health is a scapegoat for many uncomfortable political conversations. Society demands better results from mental health treatment while simultaneously reducing or cutting funding to many of the programs that mental health professionals utilize and depend on.

Still, people continue to go into the mental health field with the idealistic hope that they may assist others, even just one person, feel better.

In a system where mental health professionals are strained, not provided with the funding and tools they so urgently need, and are reliably expected to do more with less, patient care will suffer. Errors are made, and corners are cut because the proper care is not funded.

In the rare instance that funding and programs are available, they are so overwhelmed by need that waiting lists become months to years long. Overtaxed therapists make mistakes. They promise something that cannot be delivered, they miss important information and mis-diagnose clients, and they feel utterly useless at the end of the day. This leads to higher burnout rates as well as higher suicide rates among mental health professionals.

On top of the already declining population of people willing to make a career out of mental health, trained professionals are lost daily due to adverse effects of such a high stress job.

From my perspective, the leading factor to emotional collapse is feeling like we just can't make a difference. We want to be able to provide each client with everything that they need to heal, everything that they need to be successful. But the realism is that we aren't equipped with magic wands, and much of what is needed is not available.

How are we supposed to assist a homeless person with schizophrenia in becoming stable when we can't provide safe housing? How do we provide needed weekly therapy sessions when caseloads are more than two hundred clients per worker? How do we make clients feel comfortable with much-needed inpatient treatment when we know the horrible outcomes at some facilities?

As mental health professionals, we are quite aware of the flaws in the system, and we work around them the best we can. Regrettably, those left in the wake of the mental health system's shortcomings are the clients. They are those folks who finally got up the courage to ask for support and are willing to put their trust in a mental health professional, hoping that these professionals have their best interests at heart.

The truth is that we fail our clients continually because what we have to offer is lacking, and this affects clients and mental health professionals destructively. Mental health professionals fight every day to make the system better, but we can't do it alone. It will take much more than therapists saying that we need more money, it will take communities standing up and shouting that this isn't right, that it isn't enough, and that we need to do better!

And it will take those courageous enough to share their stories with the world, like Manda Jones, so that others may see how broken the system actually is.
—K.N. Lucas
Master's Degree in Counseling Psychology, LPC

AUTHOR'S NOTE

In this book I do not write with a lot of pretext. That is intentional. It should not matter what my socioeconomic status is. It should not matter what has caused the wounds that led to my need for treatment. What does matter is that mental health services should be available for everyone. We should not continue the practices of understaffing, providing minimal inpatient therapy, geographical access obstructions to mental healthcare, underpaying our mental healthcare service providers, and giving them impossible caseloads.

Defeating My Demons is written in the context of how I experienced my world during a mental breakdown. The book is about my authentic emotional journey, and others' affairs are for their hand to write.

In the moment, my mother did not provide me with what I needed. I know in a clearer headspace that her way of supporting me is to and make me feel better.

"Honey, you need to do something to get your mind off of this." My mother's monotone comment caused me to throw the phone to the ground.

I found her reactions inconsiderate and missing the seriousness of the situation. She attempted to offer support in her way, but the circumstances; beyond her. I needed professional guidance. Doing her best as a mother, she was trying to deescalate me.

Like most girls, I idolize my dad. However, we have always had a problematic relationship. Our difficulties should not be construed as either one of us having any malice. He is a good man, a man of his word, a quiet and principled man. His story is for him to write. But the burden that his internal skirmishes put on me is part of my story, and that is the part that I will.

Being a child of an alcoholic does not end when you move out on your own. It is lingering self-doubt and anxiety from years of mental chaos. I must face it, forgive it, and let it go. Crawling up that mountain, however, takes time. I also process things meticulously, which is time-consuming. This is how my mind works, and I must respect this.

I am more sensitive than I let on. My walls come down for a few human beings. Rejection and judgment are two of the rawest emotions for me. Learning to speak out can be liberating.

"This is the story you will write!" Jason looked at me as he opened the door of Dillard Manor to set me free.

Claiming brave and telling this story was terrifying. It would be dishonest to allege writing this book was not; I still have that bubble of fear sitting in the middle of my chest. Facing that fear is where the bravery marches in.

"Manda, someday you need to write a story, an experience, you have the talent and the experiences." Words my grandma Bonnie spoke to me during my senior year of high school. Those words stick with me today. Maybe this is not the story she expected. However, I hope it brings her joy to see our fifteen-year-old conversation coming to fruition.

I hope that reading my story will validate others who have had similar involvement or who are underwhelmed by the current state of the United States' mental healthcare system.

I would also like you to think about those folks in our society who cannot afford mental health care or Intensive Outpatient Programs. Some people do not have the right insurance, resources, or support available to them. Rural communities may have few to no mental healthcare providers. Some people don't have a voice because they are already underwater.

We cannot fix what we do not acknowledge, and the state of healthcare in the United States needs to change before we lose more loved ones to the mental health crisis plaguing our country.

My story is raw, upsetting, perhaps hard to read, and honest. Jason's viewpoint and mine are documented in this story to give context to what became our experience in January 2019.

Judge less and empower more.

DEFEATING MY DEMONS

Manda Jones

BREAKDOWN

*Although my windows got a view, where the frame
I'm looking through seems to have no concern for me.*
—*Jack Johnson*
(BREAKDOWN)

The year 2018 broke me in two. Not a breach, rather a complex fracture. Pieces went missing, making the whole impossible to re-configure. The crack already there became a chasm such that separation; unavoidable and irreversible.

It began meek enough with a wedge lung biopsy. This surgery entailed the surgeon taking a wedge of my right lung out for biopsy and review through several laparoscopic incisions. A chest tube required post-op to drain blood and fluid from the intrusion of the surgery.

My sweet mother–in–law and father–in–law, Sandy and Doug, drove the three hours from Kansas to our home in Colorado to get me to surgery by 5:00 in the morning while my husband, Jason, took the kids to school. Jason joined us at the hospital after he dropped the kids off, as did my sister-in-law.

Our oldest son eleven at the time, our twin boys ten, and our daughter just eight-years-old. They are a handful to rush out the door each morning. Sandy knew every detail of the ordeal after raising four children herself.

Folks with the flu had swamped the hospital, and the hospital staff struggled to find a room for me post-op. Doug and Sandy had to hop on the road back to their farm in Kansas. So, they snuck into the recovery room,

"Sweety it is going to be okay." Sandy teared up as she rubbed my arm.

"We have to go back to the farm, though I hate leaving you without getting you to a room first." Sandy continued as I cried from the pain of the chest tube.

Doug was pretty quiet, but his presence meant a lot. He is a man of action not words. Sandy hugged me gently and walked out of the room. Doug and Sandy had gotten into recovery to say good-bye under the ruse that they were my parents. That was the only way that Doug and Sandy could get into the recovery room, against protocol. Hearing Sandy call me her daughter made my heart melt, although we rarely spoke the words, I know that she loved me and I her. We were both guarded. However, at times we could let those walls down and have deep and meaningful conversations late into the night.

It drove Jason and Doug banana's when Sandy and I would stay up into the early morning hours. "Clucking" away, as Doug described it.

The evening ended in a hospital room that had somehow been found, with Jason and my brother–in–law, Bruce and his wife Sherry visiting. I held a pillow firmly to my chest because Jason and Bruce made me laugh so hard. Those two always had me in stitches. Laughing with a chest tube and several incisions requires some finesse.

I may have only had a chest tube after the wedge lung biopsy for twenty-four hours, but darn plenty for me! Having that tube removed was one of those medical moments that I would not soon forget. It whistled as it rapidly ripped from my upper chest. My insides felt as if they got sucked out with it.

I had wanted to wait for Jason to be present before removing the tube. Terrified, and of course, YouTube made it look scary. However, the doctor, in a rush to discharge me, wanted to remove the tube post haste.

The doctor sent me home on a low-dose narcotic called Tramadol. *I had been sick since childhood and knew this would not be sufficient.*

I had been on morphine as a patient in the hospital, but the doctor expected me to be fine recovering with insufficient medication.

I understood the reality of the opioid crisis in this country. But in my humble opinion, certain situations warrant the use of narcotics, one of which is an open–body–cavity surgical wound. My primary care physician was able to curb my discomfort by the following day responsibly. *Luckily, he saw me the day after surgery, between patients, because of his working knowledge of my body and my other ailments.*

Interstitial lung disease, just my newest diagnosis, in 2015. After a bronchoscopy, the pulmonologist found stomach acid in my lungs. A bronchoscopy is a scope that goes down your throat while under anesthesia and can take biopsies from the lungs without external intrusions.

I then had a Nissen fundoplication surgery in 2016 to prevent my stomach contents from being aspirated due to severe GERD. Nissen Fundoplication surgery, a surgery that fixes Hiatal hernias and then stitches the stomach around the esophagus to prevent further aspiration.

I had suffered from GERD my entire life, so I was puzzled about how long my stomach acid had been scarring up my lungs.

I found out there was something wrong on the heels of reproductive surgeries because my blood oxygen level was being checked so regularly at appointments and surgeries. Mine were low every check. My primary care physician, Dr. Jade, and I discussed this new development and had an Xray done of my lungs.

At the follow-up appointment Dr. Jade said my lungs looked like "ground glass."

As she explained, I didn't hear it. Dr. Jade referred me to the pulmonologist that did lung surgery in 2015. It was a scary and dark time for me. *Another WIN for my ailments and a big fat zero for me!* My lungs continued to worsen, and my insurance changed providers.

In 2018 my new pulmonologist performed the Wedge Lung Biopsy. *This also meant that I would have to change primary care physicians and sadly had to leave Dr. Jade's care.*

After the bronchoscopy, the pulmonologist discovered the stomach acid in my lungs and the scar tissue that erosion had left behind. This time the pulmonologist had to take a piece out of the side of my lung, the pulmonologist had to go in through my right side through four incisions and cut a wedge out of my lung for biopsy. Some of the tests required being sent to New York City for definite finding.

The conclusion: I had collagen thickening in my lungs, to the best of my understanding, created by an autoimmune response. The constant attack from my body on my lungs caused the collagen thickening.

Although scientifically, the pulmonologist had figured out another piece of the puzzle, this did not provide relief from the mental agony of having another condition to fight or a plan of action.

Surgeries like the Nissen Fundoplication I discussed above, where they tie my esophagus around my stomach to prevent stomach acid aspiration, failed. Had that been successful need for further treatment and surgeries may have been unnecessary. Unfortunately, because of the episodes of incessant vomiting the pressure and trauma had loosened the Nissen Fundoplication inside of me.

I had a diagnosis that I did not understand, nor did I know how to treat interstitial lung disease. But I had inhalers and supplemental oxygen! It seemed that my doctors wanted to treat the symptoms rather than the interstitial lung disease.

I twisted into thirty-one years old in 2018!

MOTHERHOOD IS A FIERCE JOB

*Being a mother is a fierce job.
When you see or hear your cubs being attacked,
you have an immediate internal reaction.*

In March of 2018 my thirty-first birthday came and went, and Jason and I faced the nuts and bolts of our daughter's anxiety disorder.

It had gotten to the point my child would talk to no one other than myself. She was unable by this point; she was too anxious to speak to family members, friends, and even her father.

Our daughter's anxiety consumed her to the point that she could not speak a word in class from kindergarten to second grade. Not a word. It commenced with her not being able to express herself in school, which worsened over time.

At this point, Jason and I were desperate for guidance. I had become the only person with whom our daughter would communicate. We finally landed an appointment with Children's Hospital in Aurora, Colorado, and implemented the changes that the specialist recommended. To embrace and guide our child through the diagnosis of Selective Mutism Anxiety Disorder and Gender Dysphoria. They worked, and gradually Jason and I noticed our daughter began to blossom.

By this time, many members of our family thought that our daughter was spoiled and rude. The fact that our daughter does not fit the mold others think she should, she is too complicated, and they refused to learn how; the divided mounted. *It's like one day she existed, and the next she did not. For Jason and I, that was unacceptable and at that point drew a line in the sand; if family members and friends could respect our family and treat our children equally, our response would be "kick rocks," as Jason would say.*

Love and support are what need to be offered in challenging emotive situations, not condemnation. Our daughter is the baby of the family, and that distinction does come with a certain amount of spoiling. Some family members refused to accept our child and understand the situation. That caused some divides and controversy, more because of poor communication than facts. This hardship showed Jason and me how ugly and how magnificent the world around us could be.

The ignorance displayed by some of our family members and friends during this time left me feeling vulnerable and insecure. I hoped that because my husband, my children, and I were going through many adjustments, others would be more understanding. Instead, I just felt more condemnation and loneliness. I often wondered why those close to me had such strong opinions about my parenting. On the basis that our child was not up to par for them, we have been repeatedly taken aside or just plain ignored.

The parenting of our children may have seemed different because we are adoptive parents. Our children came home as babies. However, the process of adopting them involved a long time fostering them. It took some time for the parental rights of their birth parents to be terminated for all of them.

Our children had suffered with trauma responses. This requires a different parenting philosophy. Many biological parents did not understand this.

By October 2018, the heaviness of my life was drilling into my head. Due to both my physical health problems and my mental health issues, I had been dealing with crippling depression for more than three years. *Debilitated to the point that I was sometimes not able to do anything but sleep, I did not eat, I did not give a damn, and felt like I was drowning and failing life. I gave up on sex and communication in my marriage. I stopped being supermom. I stopped. Everyone else seemed to be zooming by why I stood still paralyzed.*

The holidays had always been hard for me, but that year it was brutal. I could not manage to pull my brain away from its demons. I wanted distance from existence, even if that meant making people not want to be around me.

The day before Thanksgiving, I made Jason's life a living hell. Patient and kind, he did not deserve the venom that I hurled his way, but a switch had been flipped, and I could not hold back. Like the stoic figure he always is, he waited for me to return to my right mind before approaching me to discuss the bone that I had picked with him.

I do not even recall what I spewed at him, but I reflect on the hurt that I saw in his eyes. That is part of what brought me out of my fit.

I do not always understand Jason's patience with me, but I am always grateful for it.

UNDERWATER IN JUDGEMENT

Instead of using narcotics for the pain associated with colitis and interstitial cystitis, I used cannabis. I live in Colorado, where the purchase and use of cannabis is legal, which is fabulous for me because narcotics notoriously deteriorated my health when used to curb the agony I went through daily.

For Christmas in 2018, we spent our vacation with Jason's family. With Sandy fighting stage four Small Cell Lung Cancer, the family intended to spend as much quality time with her as possible. During the trip, one member of the family called me out for taking care of my afflictions by using cannabis. *I disapprove of your lifestyle*, the language used to express his sentiments.

I stood up for myself in a wishy-washy way. "I don't remember asking your permission."

Inside, my heart hurt, and I escaped to my room to lament. In the cabin we were staying in, each couple had their own bedrooms and the kids had a lot of rooms upstairs to sleep. But this time was no different than the thousands of other times that I had sobbed. I had cried every single day since May, and now I found myself in December. I found myself in a familiar place, feeling like those close to me were judging me. My insecurity was all-consuming. It did not matter if what someone else thought about me was true. It was my perception that counted.

I did not start off using cannabis until the age of twenty-eight, so I felt misunderstood. I decided to talk about it on that vacation, hoping that I might re-frame the discussion about cannabis and do my best to lessen the stigma surrounding cannabis with my family.

The rest of the trip sucked. The interstitial lung disease proved that it would no longer allow me to breathe well at 8,000 feet; Granby, Colorado, is a fabulous and stunning place. However, my body just was not ready for this kind of trip. The elevation led to low energy and the need to sleep a lot. I felt guilty that I could not participate in sledding, hot cocoa, exploration of the woods, the snow-covered mountains where the sunshine reflected in beautiful beams of light, that my kids and my nieces and nephew frolicked in and soaked up.

Granby, Colorado, is a beautiful place, and the cabin in which we stayed was humongous and stunning. *Close your eyes and picture the snow-covered Rocky Mountains. Watching the sunshine bouncing off the snow in every clearing available to it. Steep hills are made by nature for your children to enjoy. As close to heaven that I will ever be.* Sandy, suffering from terminal cancer, had to leave one day into the trip, as the elevation caused her physical distress. Her cancer, a battle that consumed the entire family.

Cabin in Granby, CO where we spent our final Christmas with Sandy. 2018

A couple of weeks after our return home from the vacation, my parents visited. My primary trigger walked through my front door, as the grandpa of the year. The first time that I had seen or spoken to my father in a year, and I was glad to see him. My mother came prepared with all of the gear necessary to spoil her grandbabies rotten. She and the kids baked and baked.

The kids were in awe of the crossbows that they received from their grandparents. My sons loved playing cards with their grandpa, as I had done throughout my childhood. I enjoyed playing cards as an adult as well. Spades is reminiscent of playing partners with my father and his friends. I always got first pick for a partner and nine out of ten times, I chose my dad. Then there was Pitch with grandpa. We would sit around his little card table and play cards for hours. *That card table was now mine, rusty and on the older side, but one of my most prized possessions.*

"Don't dog-ear those cards." He would jokingly say as he taught me to shuffle and bridge the cards.

My father and I also played Gin Rummy often, and it got competitive as my skill grew. The game War reminds me of my brother TJ. I got my first big talking about cheating as a young girl playing War with TJ because I had just been throwing the same Ace out every time. TJ was around three or four, so hold judgments on that front. My father does not raise his voice, but you knew it by the look in his eye, it was severe, and I never cheated at cards again.

RETURN TO THE PAST

My inner child in distress

I love my dad. He is a funny and kind man when sober. He is also an alcoholic.

The first night at our home he went to the local liquor store with my husband and picked up a case of his favorite, Coors Light. He drank throughout the evening and into the night. He drank to the point of being wasted, and my mother, my kids, my husband, and my sister had already retired for the night.

This left me alone with my dad in the kitchen. He had drank most of his thirty-pack of his Coors Light.

Even the site of those cans makes my chest feel tight and my mind to race.

Everyone had retired to bed because he was continuing to get more and more intoxicated. They did not want to be a part of it. However, I am a people pleaser, and I love my dad; I wanted to spend time with him. That was my mistake in the situation. My kind and humble father morphed into a mean, hateful, and dismissive person.

Dad did not agree with a big part of my parenting decisions or raising of the children. Often had more kind things to say about my husband, but spiteful things about me. He and my brother agreed with their judgments of our parenting. However, they never called it "our" decisions. My immediate family commonly regarded "bad" choices as solely mine as if I held Jason against his will. When confronted with that, Jason had been known just to ghost you from his life. For if you were to think anyone controlled Jason's thoughts, they did not know Jason to begin with. Dad refused to respect the guidelines Jason and I had established moving forward, as did my brother.

I did not think that he would have such venom towards his grandchildren and myself. In my heart, I know that is not the real him; in his right mind, he loved them fully.

He broke my heart for the millionth time. Hate was coming out of his mouth, hate that I did not want to hear from my dad. However, I knew he was capable of saying hateful things under the influence. That was my tipping point.

The moment that little girl inside me came out and chaos consumed my mind. I was like a robot for the rest of the time they were at my home. I just fell back into that sad and pitiful role of protector. Protector of both him and everyone else under my roof. I did not tell Jason what he had said until my parents took off back to Eastern Kansas. I knew if my husband knew, he would make my father leave by force. There is nothing more I hate when I am overwhelmed with those emotions then confrontation.

I could no longer hold back the lump in my throat. When the tears flowed grudgingly, no matter how hard I tried to hold them in, a glimpse of my sober dad appeared. My tears caused him to weep as well. He hugged me, then like time had been lost, he reverted to being vicious. In those gentle moments where tears flowed, you could see he wanted to support me, but he could not bring himself to complete that journey.

Why surprised? I did not know. But I felt broken. I managed to put him to bed and hand him off to my mother and rushed downstairs to the spare bedroom. I bawled for what felt like an eternity until I finally drifted off to sleep.

The next day I had to don the *Manda face*. I pretended that life was fine, even though inside, I was so upset that I felt like that little girl who just wanted her dad's support and love. I could not bring myself to talk about what I was feeling.

I felt so broken, helpless, and alone when he talked about my children in such a way, even as I was trying to explain, he did not listen to a word I said like we were in parallel universes. The smell of his chew, the noise of a beer can opening, his language, and hate. In my eyes, he was mocking my family.

Clockwise: Shooting the crossbows my children were gifted from their grandma and grandpa Jones. Manda and her grandfather 2004. Manda dancing with her father to 'I Loved Her First' by Heartland, January 6, 2007. Jason and Sandy dancing at our wedding, January 6, 2007.

Clockwise: Manda and her mother, Sherry, 1987. Manda and her eldest son Austin getting pumped up for this quarterbacks football game! Manda and her daughter Zay, bringing in the New Year at a little French restaurant. Girls and their filters! Manda and her son Jessy hanging out in the shade on a family camping trip having a conversation about life, 2020. Manda and her son Nicklas competing for family bowling champ! 2020.

TAKING OFF THE MASK

I did not tell a soul until two days after their departure. I lost it!

I was off my rocker in a way that scared Jason enough to take me to Dillard Manor, a mental health hospital, where I signed a voluntary 72–hour hold. Did I need help? Yes. Suicidal? Indeed. I had hit a mental brick wall where I thought that being alive could be worse for my children than me dying. I felt that the kids would be better off being raised by Jason's family, that my family was unwell, and that I needed to break the cycle.

What others felt about my parenting was none of my business until voiced to me. When I hit my breaking point, I felt like the cycle of alcoholism, hateful actions and words, broken promises, verbal abuse, would never stop unless I severed that tie.

My mind was taking me to the depths of hades. The place my mind took me to, that I needed to stop the cycle and keep my children away from family and friends that do not accept them. When my children are not enough to pull me back, I am in trouble and need help. I was headed down a stigmatized road, looked down upon, and some say a coward's way out. *I can tell you it is no cowards way out. It is a deep pain. It is despair you do not feel you have the strength to overcome. It is being unable to get out of bed and seeing the quality of your life slipping.*

I was ready to die. I did not reach out to anyone for support during this dark time. Instead, I retreated into myself.

And so began the next phase of my downward spiral.

Not only did I suffer from general anxiety disorder, post-traumatic stress disorder, and depression, I also agonized with interstitial lung disease, interstitial cystitis, colitis, endometriosis, polycystic ovarian syndrome, non-alcoholic fatty liver disease, GERD, gastritis, cyclic vomiting syndrome, arthritis, pelvic floor dysfunction, gastric emptying complications, and chronic pain.

I do not share this to gain sympathy; rather, I am stating the facts. Dealing with all this happened to be my truth.

I cannot count the number of procedures, surgeries, ER visits, and hospital stays over the last decade or the amount of money we were billed. It is an overwhelming reality and something that Jason and I tackled daily. Jason's truth is that he had a chronically ill wife who could feel great to being hospitalized in one day. He had to take time off work, take care of the kids, house, bills, basically be a single dad; he too was at a breaking point between my attitude, four kids, and trying to keep us financially on track.

The way that the healthcare system works in the United States has become frightening for people like me, and I am here to share my story.

My journey to help was not voluntary, I ignored what was happening, and I did not seek help or support. However, when you throw a chronically sick human being, in the middle of a tremendous flare-up, into a room for three days, and throw away the key, bad things can happen. I could not get my required oxygen for night due to my interstitial lung disease; my blood oxygen levels drop into the 70's when I sleep, so I need 2.5 liters of oxygen when I sleep. (Blood oxygen levels should be above 90.) This, when taking Ambien and Xanax in the hospital, is unsafe. They finally got it to me on the second night of my stay. There were others with more severe conditions than I that said they had been there five or six days, and you cannot get everything you need until around day three.

I do not control my pain with opioids. However, in the hospital or Emergency Room, I do not have an option.

Sometimes the doctor is great, the ones that would listen to my standard protocol and give the medications I needed to get my vomiting and pain under control. Then some had no respect for me. However, every time I had to go in, I panicked. When a doctor asked what I need to get it under control, I was afraid to speak up because doctors treat almost everyone like a drug addict. I got lucky occasionally and got my favorite nurses; I could tell them I need Dilaudid, Phenergan, fluids, and a potassium drip to start. The three or four ER nurses that knew me relayed to the doctors what my conditions were.

I have said every trip to the emergency room was a year off my life. I was afraid they would judge me and write me off, fearful of the extreme amount of radiation my body has been exposed to via x-Ray's, CT Scans, and MRI's. Afraid I would get a nurse who did not know how to access my port and probe my arm with a needle while the nurses chase the ultrasounds findings.

Sometimes they used Ketamine. It was much worse than narcotics for me. For me, it was like being in a tunnel I could not escape from, and you cannot see the surrounding that you already witnessed being there. The dignity of the patients had been disappearing for some time and of no importance to hospitals.

I SNAPPED, HE SNAPPED

Jason expressed something harmless,
but it triggered me and set me off,
and down the rabbit hole I scampered.
I was at my breaking point.

"I am done! When my dad was here, he said some painful and ignorant things to me, and I was afraid to tell you. I thought you would rough him up."

"I am so sorry! WHY DID YOU NOT WAKE ME? Your mother did nothing? I would have had your dad sleeping on the hood of his car until she got up the next morning to drive him home!"

I think that was the point I snapped. Jason had every right to say it, damn it, I agreed with him! Yet I felt at the time that he was attacking my dad, and I was still a little girl inside trembling. Still trying to protect my family, but also protect my dad.

I may have looked calm on the outside, until this point, but inside I trembled and wanted to park myself in front of a train.

I do not remember every detail of that particular episode. I do recall calling for my mother on the bathroom floor. I look back at begging Jason not to take me to Dillard Manor and stabbing myself in the wrist with a hard object. I *believe it was the wall charger for my iPhone;* in the car with enough force, my wrist was bruised for a week. I remember parts of the drive to Dillard Manor.

At one point, I called my mother. For some reason, I needed her at that moment. I felt dismissed as I cried on the telephone. I hung up and tossed the phone on the floor of the car.

Jason drug me into Dillard Manor Mental Health Center. Someone there sent us to the emergency room at Colorado General Hospital, across the street, because Dillard Manor didn't have a crisis team. I was at the ER long enough that I had worn off the cannabis that I had eaten earlier, and I was on day four of a colitis flare-up *(I thought)*.

The stabbing in my pelvis had gotten intolerable, and Jason explained to a nurse how I treated my discomfort and that I would need a replacement for the cannabis in the hospital. The issue with the illness *(colitis)* was if left untreated caused vomiting. I had cyclic vomiting syndrome, a condition where I was unable to stop throwing up without interventions. I had medication at home for nausea, but it did not always work. If we missed the early intervention, the retching would start to tear up my esophagus, leading to bleeding in addition to the electrolyte imbalance that came with losing that much fluid. Half the time that lead to a hospital stay where pain and vomiting were controlled intravenously with medication and supplemental potassium and magnesium. My potassium could get critically low within a few hours of when the episode began. I was aware I had a fifty percent chance of needing to move to a medical hospital if throwing up started.

After the nurse had communicated my conditions to the doctor, the nurse returned from her quick conversation with the ER doctor that I was assigned to. The doctor ordered medication then and there and gave me nausea and pain medication via the IV port in my chest.

I had had a port in my chest since 2015. My veins had been beaten up throughout my life because of mounting health issues. During a routine scope a surgeon lost access to my veins because the IV blew *(where your vein collapses and the IV catheter is then unable to let medications flow through or blood draw out,)* and the anesthesiologist struggled to get a new line started, combined with the fact my veins were small and unreliable. The time before a port was decided on was a harrowing medical experience. The nursing staff for my ECT treatments dug at my veins eleven tries: zero success. This episode ended when the nursing staff finally got a working IV in my ankle! PICC-line and Mid-line's had lasted only hours to a day on average. *PICC-line and Mid-lines are IVs placed in the upper arm using ultrasound guidance, and the catheter is much longer and leads to just above the heart.*

My surgeons and primary physicians decided that I needed a permanent port for access. A port is a device implanted under your skin near your collarbone. It is tapped into a major artery. All nurses and anesthesiologists had to do is access it with a special needle, and then I could receive medication, and blood work could be done from there. As much as I disliked it, I realized its extraordinary benefits.

My intake at Dillard Manor was done via video chat. A woman appeared on the screen and began to talk to me about the concerns I had about going into Dillard Manor? *What concerns didn't I have? I knew that going into the hospital without a guarantee that medication replacement would happen, I wanted it ordered before I entered! I could be trapped in pain during a colitis flare that could cause a medical nightmare or hospitalization, a reality facing me. I expressed this is so many words; she seemed to be listening. I soon learned accountability is not a priority for Dillard Manor. The woman on the screen made promises that I was skeptical about. What was the alternative? Under the impression, I may be placed on an involuntary hold. I also expressed the concern of my medications being kept on schedule and given to me. I had two nerve pain medications that were necessary for me. Several other medications were less dire but still needed to be maintained.*

Up to that time, I had been coping with chronic pain and flare-ups by using edible medical marijuana twice a day. However, I knew that I wouldn't be allowed to have cannabis inpatient and that I would have to rely on narcotic (opioid) medications to relieve the agony.

Scared in a way, Jason had a separate conversation with this woman to emphasize that Dillard Manor's medical staff could not let the pain get out of control. With her pledge that the anguish would be dealt with, I signed my life away.

Jason left me at Colorado General, waiting for transport to Dillard Manor across the street. He wanted to stay with me, but he had to pick our children up from school.

When transport showed up, a nurse walked into the hospital room at Colorado General to remove the needle from my port, severing any access for medications for me. That nausea and pain would start to creep back in without medication. *Was Dillard Manor going to allow pain medication?*

WHAT THE HELL DID I JUST SIGN-UP FOR?

Unprepared for the Terror Ahead

Protocol at Colorado General dictated that I have a safe hospital room where I could not access anything to harm myself. A security guard kept watch to ensure my safety. The emergency room staff at Colorado General also made me change into paper scrubs for my safety. I stayed at Colorado General for three to four hours from arrival to transport to Dillard Manor.

My nurse entered my room to escort me into the hallway, where the security guard assigned to watch me handed my belongings to an older gentleman in uniform. This man never looked at me or spoke; he grabbed my belongings from the security guard and stormed off. "Sorry, follow him." The security guard stuttered.

After the gentleman in uniform gestured for me to crawl in the backseat of a car, he then plunked himself into the driver's seat.

"You do realize that I am literally driving you across the street, right?" the gentleman grunted.

I could not blame him for being annoyed. It was a stone's throw from Colorado General to Dillard Manor. Being an inpatient mental health facility, Dillard Manor should have had a crisis team, but they did not. A crisis team is in place to keep those who have a mental health crisis stay safe while the medical providers determine whether hospitalization is necessary.

I apologized. He ranted throughout the short drive. Here I was on one of the worst days of my life, in paper scrubs in the backseat of a security car on my way to a mental health facility for inpatient care, and I was apologizing for inconveniencing an on-duty security person meant to keep me safe?

This is my fresh hell. I wanted to smack him in the head with a 2 x 4.

After I arrived at Dillard Manor, a couple of random nurses led me into a room and quizzed me, expecting answers to a long series of questions. The nurses kept switching from one of them to the other. In front of them, they had me change from the Colorado General issued paper scrubs to the new scrubs that they wanted me to wear on their unit. Jason was able to bring me some sweats to wear instead of the scrubs the next day. Outside clothing was allowed if the patient's clothing had no drawstrings and was inspected by hospital staff.

Time and again, I pleaded, "I need you to read my medical files, please. I am going to need help managing these symptoms."

Dismissively, "There is no doctor here tonight."

"I was told that I would be receiving medical care as soon as I arrived here?" I said, feeling myself shut down my emotions.

They simply looked through me as if I were saying nothing at all, I indicated that the medication that I had been given at Colorado General across the street would last until morning, but I would need to keep on top of the pain. If the physical agony escalated, I knew that I would be in a harrowing situation.

"Kriston, the woman who did my intake, she promised I would see a doctor right away." I tried to assert through the lump in my throat.

"Please, call Kriston!"

With the dismissive nature of the nurses, I felt unable to speak up any further. Defeat lingered. I panicked. Someone, or more than one someone, had lied to me.

I saw at that point that no communication between Kriston and the medical staff at Dillard Manor, whom I believed Kriston worked for, had occurred.

Kriston was never seen or heard from again. Jason never prevailed trying to contact Kriston after their first phone call while still at Colorado General, when she assured him that my medical issues would be treated. On the inside, I was unable to get anyone to listen. I insisted to these two nurses that I needed to see the doctor as soon as possible in the morning. I spelled out for them in no uncertain terms that the strain was under control for the time being but that that would not last.

The nurses took me on a tour of the facility and led me past a room in which sat a television, and coloring books and half-finished puzzles covered a table there. They then directed me down a hallway and pointed out the lunchroom/classroom. Then they showed me my room, a private room, the first positive sign that I had seen since I arrived at Dillard Manor. Those haughty nurses then left me for the night to cry myself to sleep.

I recall calling Jason, "Kriston lied to us; they have no idea what my medical conditions are!" I cried on the phone.

Shocked, "I will get to the bottom of this, Manda! I promised you would be taken care of." You could hear the defeat in his cracking voice.

"They took advantage of us; they will not help me, and I am scared."

The following morning, Jason was on the horn first thing trying to track down Kriston, proved harder than he thought. This Kriston person did not even seem to be a real human being who worked at Dillard Manor, or else everyone who worked there had somehow all forgotten about her. The doctor that Kriston promised that I would see was not real either. All of the nurses had zero ideas about my pre-existing medical conditions, even though Kriston had asserted that my medical charts would be available to doctors and staff and that I would be well cared for.

From where I stood, we had been entirely dismissed. I had been lied to, to manipulate me into signing the voluntary commitment.

Dillard Manor gained five thousand dollars for the 72-hours I was dumped in a room, in writhing pain and unable to eat for three days. In addition to the $1200 for the ER visit to Colorado General, both hospitals were owned by the same cooperation. I had no idea how much the treatment was going to cost going in. I found out how much I was charged for inpatient care when I received a statement from my insurance company. I thought that I was paying to obtain the establishment of aid for myself, for the sake of my family and me. Instead, locked up and tormented.

In fact, as Dr. S., the physiatrist in charge, and the staff at Dillard Manor rushed to discharge me on the last day of my 72-hour hold, he apologized for traumatizing me!

What the nurses and care coordinators – I could not define their fundamental role in my care – and patient advocates had done could not be justified. Dr. S., to his credit, was honest and divulged the failures of himself, the nurses, the patient advocates, three care coordinators, and the therapists at Dillard Manor. I could see in his eyes and hear in his voice that he felt he had failed. You could see that he was overburdened and unable to meet his patients' needs because he was alone in this with two patients' wings. It was not a lack of desire to help every one of us, that was clear in his body language and tone. He was sorry, but I was traumatized, dammit!

Intake into Dillard Manor was just the beginning what proved to be a real dangerous medical issue for me. What I have related above constitutes what happened on just my first night at Dillard Manor.

The people that I met, they needed a voice. They needed a fierce and protective husband on the phone all day screaming at doctors and care coordinators to gain results. The injustices that I saw made me cringe in horror.

They needed what I had. Even with my support, I had been unable to get the help I required. I should have been sent back to Colorado General Hospital.

Something was wrong with this picture because my vex could not be controlled.

I did not find out that I had been suffering from much more than a colitis flare-up until the Intensive Outpatient Program. I had a CDiff or Clostridium difficile infection. CDiff is a bacterium that naturally resides in our intestines. However, when it grows out of control, it causes severe illness. At the end of March 2019, a doctor finally checked for the most obvious first and found a terrible infection. She believed that I got it after a root canal in December 2018 that required antibiotics.

JASON'S FIGHT

Jason Bjorn

I was supposed to begin my two-week rotation on nights on the day that Manda snapped. She started to lose it in the car. I didn't understand the root of her anger, but Manda was pissed. She echoed over and over that she was done...full stop.

We parked in our driveway after returning home from the grocery store. I strode into the house to escape the meltdown. Manda sat out in the car for a time by herself.

She finally returned inside, grabbed a suitcase, and yelled, "I'm going to see my mom!"

Going to her mom's didn't make sense to me. I knew that this could be a poor idea on several levels. Her parents were the main reason for this wreck and driving twelve hours to see them would have made it worse. Two, Manda was having problems with her car, so she planned to take my pickup. That would have left me home alone with four kids and no vehicle.

"Nonsense", I thought.

She then marched into the bathroom to gather her toothbrush and other essentials. I grabbed her just to hold her and told her that I did not think that seeing her mom was a brilliant idea at that time. She fell to the ground and sobbed. She slammed her arm into a cabinet door.

"Manda, I'm taking you to the mental hospital! This is out of control!" My fear got the better of me.

Manda refused.

I held my ground. "Sweetheart, the people there will assist you. I promise. I'll make sure of it."

As I made this vow to Manda, I used the awesome Google machine to find a hospital close to home and read some reviews. I found two—one in Greeley, Colorado, and one in Fort Collins, Colorado. Neither had stellar reviews, so I chose the best of the worst, which scored a 2.7 out of five stars. Ratings were not excellent, but it was better than the other, and Manda was in crisis.

I finally convinced Manda to hop into the pickup, and we drove to Fort Collins, roughly twenty-five miles away. The kids, luckily, still at school. Manda's breakdown happened early enough in the day that I could make the thirty-minute drive to Fort Collins and get Manda checked in before rushing home to gather the kids.

As I drove to Ft. Collins, Manda sobbed the entire thirty-minutes. She called her mom, and two minutes into the conversation, she hung up. Of course, her mom called her back, but Manda refused to answer, so her mother called me.

"Manda needs help. I'm taking her to the hospital. I'll update you when I can." My tinny voice spoke to the precarious condition of my nerves.

I also somehow managed to text my boss, just three hours before I was supposed to be on location to let him know that I would not be there that night as a fracking consultant for an oil and natural gas extraction company. My presence is not easily replaceable on the job. My boss was a wonderful and understanding man.

I parked in the parking lot at Dillard Manor Mental Health Center, and then I had to persuade Manda to get out of the pickup and enter Dillard Manor. I spent ten minutes just getting Manda out of the truck. I finally coaxed her to the front door.

I approached the lady at the front desk.

"Ma'am, my wife here is in trouble. She's losing her mind. Really. She needs professional support." I spoke softly to maintain Manda's privacy.

"I'm sorry, we do not have a crisis team here. You need to go to the emergency room across the street to find a crisis team." This arrogant woman held her nose quite high in the air.

This pissed me off. An hour into this thing by then and this bitch was telling me that no one at that hospital could or would assist us.

"You do not have a crisis team, but you are an inpatient mental hospital?" I scoffed.

"I have already told you! If you want intake, you have to go to Colorado General across the street." She spoke loudly so that everyone in the waiting room could hear her, violating Manda's privacy in such a delicate situation.

I was pissed because I had fought hard to get Manda there. I took her to a mental hospital, and they did not have a crisis team! They couldn't evaluate her. It seemed they would not do anything for her! I do not normally refer to anyone as a "bitch", but this was beyond the pale. I saw red.

After another prolonged drama, I drove Manda around the block to the emergency room at Colorado General. I had to regurgitate the same words I had just said to the receptionist at Dillard Manor, to the staff person at the front desk what was going on.

I had to convince Manda that the doctors and nursing staff would help her, not hurt her. I didn't know at the time that I lied to her. I thought that between Colorado General and Dillard Manor, Manda would get the comprehensive support that she needed.

Colorado General, is a medical hospital, and Manda had to sign paperwork to be treated, which she showed reluctance in doing. The folks in the ER took excellent care of her. They got her pain and her anxiety under control. The ER doctor relayed that a care coordinator, Kriston, needed to see her and could do it via webcam, or she would have to wait several hours for someone to make time to evaluate her in person.

Manda opted for the webcam so that she didn't have to wait in the ER for hours longer than necessary. She spoke to Kriston via webcam, and Kriston assured Manda that the whole thing would be fine. Manda finally felt willing to go to Dillard Manor for inpatient care on a voluntary 72-hour hold.

I even had Kriston call my cell phone and leave a message for me. I was impressed with the way that she communicated with me.

I then had to leave the hospital to pick up our four children from school. Manda wanted me to call Kriston back and make sure that Dillard Manor had the capability of dealing with her other health issues and that she controlled at home without narcotics. I called Kriston on my way home to double-check, and when I reached her, she acted shocked that I would even call to check on the pain situation.

"I have assured Manda that she will be taken care of. Don't worry about it." Kriston's snippy tone left no doubt as to her attitude.

I returned the twenty-five miles home and picked our children up from school, something Manda usually does, so they knew something was going on from the moment they saw me. I then took them home to discuss with them that mommy needed help. I tried to frame it so that they knew and understood that it is not wrong to ask for support when you are suffering, mentally or physically.

PHANTOM DOCTOR

The Phantom Doctor. I didn't coin the phrase. Phantom Doctor is what the other patients called the doctors at Dillard Manor. I figured out why soon enough.

The first morning I awoke to the voice of a physician's assistant, who entered my room. I felt disoriented, to be expected in a situation such as the one in which I found myself. I described to the physician's assistant that the night before had not gone well and that promises had not been kept. I informed her that my colitis had flared up, and I described how I managed my pain and nausea with cannabis at home.

The physician's assistant scolded me.

"We don't allow cannabis here. At all. Ever. Get over it. I'll check the database to see if narcotic medication is appropriate, but don't bet on it."

I never even entertained the idea that cannabis would be allowed at Dillard Manor. Adding insult to injury, I braved more cannabis shaming.

My ache was creeping up to an alarming level, but I still had time to gain control. I urged the physician's assistant to call my primary care physician to shed more light on my medical issues because the physician's assistant had no idea what was going on in my world. She didn't have a clue that she needed to discuss pain management with me.

I met Dr. S., the psychiatrist, early that morning too. It would have been hard to know when, as there happened to be no clocks in the rooms, just in the hallway and community rooms, so I did not know the time. Dr. S. and I discussed at length that I had been through several medications over the past decade. I opened up that I had been through more than a year of Electroconvulsive Therapy (ECT), which is where an anesthesiologist and psychiatrist put you under anesthesia and shock your brain to induce a seizure to aid with depression. My psychiatrist during ECT also revealed that ECT had shown some benefits for chronic pain.

I articulated that I had completed Eye Movement Desensitization and Reprocessing (EMDR), in which the therapist had me hold a sensor in each hand and walked me through some distressing events in an attempt to process them.

"I have also attempted talk therapy, without feeling results."

"Why do you think talk therapy did not work for you?" Dr. S inquired.

"Well, I never know where to start. It is a jumble in my head. Should I start and walk through my childhood to now, or should I leave the past behind and focus on current situations? How do you leave the past behind when it still hurts? It's all confusing to me."

With a look of pity, "I will do my best to find a medication that I have hopes will help you."

Dr. S. then prescribed a medication called Remeron for depression. At first reluctant to take it, I did from January 2019 to December 2019, when it had to be changed for medical reasons. I wanted to feel better, but I did not have a ton of hope when it came to mental health medications because they have never seemed to do much for me. I had tried several throughout my adult life.

I clarified to Dr. S. that the physician's assistant stated that she would call my primary care physician and check some database, so that she could help out with getting my pain and nausea under control.

As minutes turned to hours with no relief medication, I shook with nervousness. Nauseated, I knew that throwing up was the next step in my body's breakdown. By some miracle, I only vomited once.

I would not leave my room, as my anguish rated a seven on a scale from one to ten. In a frenzy with the realization I had no control over my medical state and may not find relief. Fearful would be the appropriate description of my emotional state.

The nurses on the floor, who stopped by my room, brought my daily medications. *Every day, I must take two pills in the morning, two in the afternoon, and six pills at night. Due to the fact I was in too much discomfort to leave my room, they were bringing them to me. I also had a standing prescription to a powerful nausea medication that I could ask for at will because I had a preexisting prescription for that nausea medication.*

My morning pills arrived and inquired about the medicine for my pain management.

"The physician assistant said she was checking a database to see if she could prescribe me pain medication. Has this been done yet?"

"I do not know anything about that." My nurse replied. Afternoon pills were brought to me by a different nurse from the morning round.

Again, I pleaded, "I feel like I am being tortured. Has the physician's assistant ordered medication for me yet?"

"Not that I know of." The nurse replied.

"Could you please check?" I sobbed.

"If it were there, I would know." He snapped back at me.

"Could you please at least bring me my nausea medication again? The pain is escalating my nausea." I said in utter defeat.

I tried every position I could think of. I sat like a butterfly *(Yoga Talk)* on the floor in the corner of the room. This provided the best relief, so I wrapped myself in blankets and lowered myself into that tight corner. I cried.

I called Jason at some point, maybe more than once, some of it is a blur. That day comes back to me now in flashes.

I know that Jason and I were both fighting for support but to no avail. During a call, I recall clearly Jason stated, "I just talked to a woman named Betty, and she said she is your patient advocate…"

"I have never met a patient advocate or anyone by the name of Betty." I interrupted.

"I know Manda; I asked her point-blank—Have you ever seen Manda? Do you even know what she looks like?" Betty replied in a hesitant tone, "No, but as soon as we get off the phone, I will meet her."

"Betty had never seen you or spoken to you but says it is her top priority. I know that does nothing to validate your suffering, babe. I am sorry for that." Jason explained the circumstance at hand.

Done. I had been backed so far into a corner that my mind and body were frozen. Like a movie playing in my head as I sat there in that room in excruciating grief. Throbbing that radiated from my pelvis down my thighs and up into my ribs.

The words *It's okay, sweet girl* played over and over in my mind. I could not hear a voice but felt the warm presence of my grandfather in the room. He had been a safe place for me during his entire existence in my life. My mind searched for safety in a grim and disturbing situation.

I remember looking around the room, seeking any weapon so I could end it all. I felt like I had no way out, petrified. I knew, however, that I would have to endure this for seventy-two straight hours.

Did I sign up for this? I did not have the tools to cope with this.

Amid my emotional and physical meltdown, an older woman hesitantly entered my room. I recollect her name being Jen.

Like a caged animal, I screamed, "Yes, I am in fucking pain, and yes, I want to fucking die!"

My colitis had taken over, and my whole lower abdomen and pelvis were throbbing, excruciating. My chest was starting to feel like someone was sitting on it. That always meant that I was anxious and that the cyclic vomiting syndrome was now just a matter of time.

I wept and could not govern the fear. I shook. Out of anger, I shouted at the woman. I screamed that I needed aid, that I needed to go home if help could not be provided. I do not recall any words she said; I remember the look of bewilderment by my fear and level of discomfort.

Less than thirty minutes later, a nurse brought me a Percocet.

Really? I had been weeping and screaming in anguish all day. Only after I scolded Jen that I discovered that a pill had been on standby for me. At this point, beyond confused but grateful to have some relief. I swallowed the pill, wrapped myself in blankets, and fell asleep as the aching dulled. A cure-all it was not. The pain was by no means under control, but lowering it to a manageable level, a five, made life much easier on me.

Next, I awoke to two women entering my room. Groggy, I did not understand who they were. I deduced from their clothing and jargon that they were from human resources. The two women inquired about my pain management now that the medication was on board. I told them it was better because it was.

I had been dissociating before that bit of relief, so I was grateful for any easing of the strain at all! That is all I recall from the sleepy conversation.

It became clear to me that the doctors were too far behind on my pain and nausea treatment throughout the day. I needed additional medication and, of course, too frightened to inquire for it after the last ordeal. The throbbing ratcheted up.

I finally summoned the courage to ask why I had been given the Percocet *(narcotic medication)* after talking to Jen.

"It has been ordered since this morning." A brand new nurse told me with a perplexed look.

"I asked every single professional I saw today if the medication had been ordered and was never given it; in addition, they told me that it wasn't there."

I went from crying to fight mode in a moment's time. After practically begging every professional I saw all day for support with the illness level I was presenting with.

A flighty nitwit stared at me in disbelief. "It was ordered for you all day. You never approached the window."

"Are you fucking kidding me! *What window?* How is this even possible? Someone brought me all of my everyday medications, but I never approached a window for my pain medicine?" I felt crushed and talked with anger and spite in my voice.

The in house nurses and therapists withheld relief medication that was ordered for me, let me cry, allowed me to panic, and contemplate the end to my life all over again because I didn't go to a window that I didn't know existed? Talk about defeat.

Am I so insignificant in this world that I would be treated in such a demoralizing way? Why? How?

This is what hopelessness feels like. I remember sinking into a deep, black hole.

I thought that I had felt hopeless before, but this felt like deep despair at its finest.

I started to believe that maybe it was part of the program. I thought that maybe the theory was to break me down and then build me back up. I felt like I had unknowingly joined a bizarre cult from which I could not escape.

I began to play the part. I proceeded to the dining room and drank some juice. I gave away the rest of my meal. I did the same with every single meal the entire time at Dillard Manor.

I was still in extreme pain. If you have colitis or any inflammatory bowel disease, you will also understand that indignity is another element of these flare-ups.

By that night, my physical agony was out of hand again. I cried, unable to soothe myself. That night a therapist finally came in, the first person I remember even talking nicely to me. He guided me by coaching me in my breathing and engaging with me as the Xanax and other medications took effect, and I drifted into a light sleep. The discomfort was too intense for heavy sleeping, and I knew that I couldn't miss a dose of medication, or the agony could have become even worse. I had to make sure that I was awake to go to the window when the time came to take the pain medication.

I had zero authority over any aspect of my health care. All I had control of was getting to that window.

I knew that if I did not act the part, the staff at Dillard Manor could place me on an involuntary hold and make me stay longer. My care coordinator, Whitney, had told me so on day two.

Whitney stated that I had not been participating in my care. I tried to describe the illness I was fighting and how messed up everything had been.

"No one here is listening to me!" I was fried.

"Yes, yes, they are. You, however, are not leaving your room and participating in groups."

"I can not participate while feeling like this. It is not possible. I am very ill." I tried so hard to clear it up for her as she stared right through me.

"I am too overwhelmed for this conversation, you are not keeping me, and you need to talk to Jason, now!" I was on the defense.

Coincidentally, as she left, Jason and two of our sons entered the room. I did not want my sons to hear the conversation, so Jason requested that she call him in passing Whitney.

"The new physician's assistant is in a meeting and will be down to see you right after, Manda. Within the hour." Her tone mellowed in the presence of my husband. She exited the room and shut the door.

Jason and the children stayed for their allotted forty-five minutes, and then the door swung open with a gust.

"You are not ever allowed to have the door shut during visitation! You are over your time, and you need to leave!" Came the furious voice of a nurse.

Our ten-year-old immediately burst into tears.

Jason, already unhappy with this God-forsaken place, fired back. "I had nothing to do with closing that door. A member of the staff shut the fucking door! Get off my back!"

I knew that the man had been pushed way too damn far. He had promised me that I would be taken care of, and all he could see was the physical and mental agony. Dillard Manor was not holding up its end of the bargain, and Jason felt as defeated and hopeless as I did.

Whitney never called Jason. He did call her and couldn't reach her. Neither Jason nor I ever heard from her or saw Whitney again.

Whitney had told me that the physician's assistant would be in to see me within the hour. Desperate for a solution, I awaited his arrival in tears. I did not leave my room because I didn't want to miss him.

He never showed, and the pain continued to gain traction. As always, it progressed in my lower abdomen. When left untreated, I first feel a throbbing and stabbing in my lower back. The pain in that location effectively cuts me in two. This was normal during Colitis flares because they also sparked inflammation in my bladder. My entire pelvis would be inflamed during these flares. Then it creeps into my hips, and my hip joints begin to ache. It climbs up my sides into my rib cage. At its worst, I can feel an arthritic ache from my fingertips to the bottom of my feet.

Breathing becomes a chore, as these symptoms increase anxiety. I become irritable and bothered by the tiniest noise because even the sound's vibration is jarring at the worst of it.

My despair grew, and I plummeted to one of the darkest places I had ever found myself.

Three hours past the time that I expected the physician's assistant, I had had enough. I stumbled my way to the nurses' station to demand to see the physician's assistant. The nurse on duty stated that she would check to see if he was still there!

"What? I was under the impression that we had an appointment!" My fury exploded.

Fortunately, the physician's assistant was still there. He ordered an additional dose of Percocet between already-prescribed doses with the hope of breaking the pain cycle. His plan would have worked had the nurse not decided, after he left, that she did not feel comfortable giving me the doses, as prescribed, so close together (even though the quantities were ordered in such a way to work together). I was not able to curb the agony until after discharge...more than 72 hours!

WHY WAS I SO SICK?

*Flares are always terrible,
but this one took the cake*

I was hospitalized in Dillard Manor at the beginning of January 2019, and, as I mentioned before, I was finally diagnosed with a C. diff infection in March 2019. The C. diff was relentless, and even after my diagnosis, the first round of high-powered antibiotics had no impact. I responded to the second round of antibiotics and was thought to be cured.

This was not true, and I ended up battling this infection into August 2019 with three total hospital stays from June 2019 to August 2019. The average hospital stay ranged from six to ten days, and I did require one transfer to a different hospital.

In the end, after battling the infection for at least nine months, I had to have a fecal transplant to cure the infection.

There had been nothing more humbling to me than to see the shadowy figure of a nurse hovering over you telling you to fight. Hearing them tell the EMT's before transfer that I was bradycardic, and my heart needed monitored closely!

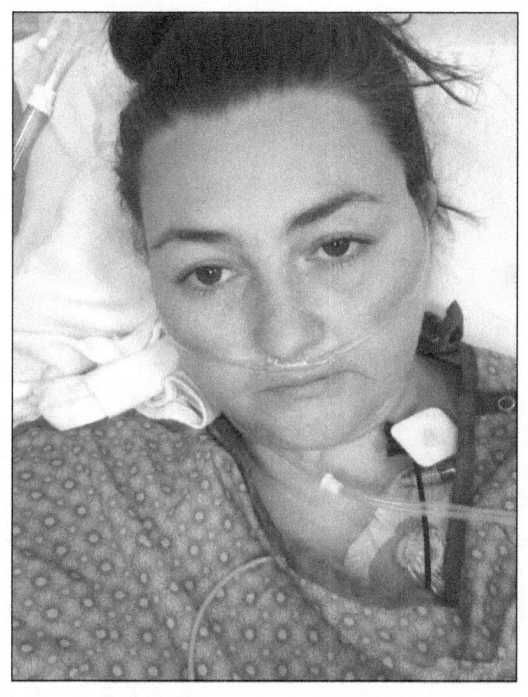

Manda during a ten-day hospital stay. Loveland, Colorado in June 2019.

MY PRIVILEGE REVELATION

Everyone's story matters

Inpatient, the elements that messed with me, the conversations and observations that made me see the world in a different light, were the people I met there. The other patients and the mountains that they too had to climb just to have the privilege of having their basic needs met boggled my mind.

I struggled even getting the supplemental oxygen of 2.5 liters that I used at night because of my interstitial lung disease, until the second night. I needed narcotics and oxygen. That's it. These simple needs seemed to be too much for the staff at Dillard Manor to handle.

I met a woman who had a crippling physical injury due to a collagen disorder. She would easily suffer more injuries if she did not acquire the needed braces and equipment to hold her body together and prevent ligaments' tearing. It took her three days to obtain the necessary support devices, such as braces for her neck and ankles, and a special wheelchair to adjust her body more gently.

"Give it a few days. Usually, by day four, you will have what you need. Until then, it is just really hard." Cheryl, my peer, told me as she lay in her wheelchair.

I remember thinking, "how in the hell is this acceptable?"

Negligent doesn't begin to cover the injustice and humiliation that I saw inflicted in that prison-like environment.

During a conversation in the "classroom" area with some of my peers, a young woman named Ann truly spoke to my heart.

"I guess I am crazy, I actually voluntarily committed myself," Ann spoke in a meek voice.

"Not silly or crazy at all, I did the same." I confessed.

"My boyfriend and I were clean and went on a binder. We are alcoholics and homeless. But I want to be clean, so I checked myself in." Tears began to form in both our eyes.

"Where will you go after this?" I inquired.

"We will go back to the streets for now and try to remain clean. I want what you have. We want to have a home and children someday." Ann asserted.

Ann was a gorgeous and kind soul. Long beautiful black hair, glowing skin, happy disposition, a person worthy of respect and dignity, and a helping hand. Someone with a goal toward change without the resources to accomplish it.

Towards the end of our first conversation, I discovered that Ann and I were the same age. I was shocked. She seemed so much younger like she had held on to her youthful spirit.

I found myself jealous of her youth that I felt I had somehow lost. Yet, I knew that when I left, I had a husband and four children that were going to embrace me in love, I was going to sleep in my bed, and I did not have an alcohol addiction to fight tooth and nail to overcome.

I also was not homeless. The fact that homeless humans are tossed back into the street after inpatient care or detox did not seem like a very sound system for mental health treatment.

"I was used in sex trafficking as a teen and young woman. After I got too old, I was pushed into stripping. Then I ran from that life and found my boyfriend. He is my soul mate, and I want a real-life with him." Ann stated.

When she made this statement, she appeared embarrassed and ashamed of her past. *It hurt my heart to know that she felt such shame over things she could not control, events forced upon her. She did not seem to realize she was the victim. She instead seemed to own it all. You could almost witness the weight of the world pushing down on her shoulders. I hope she gets all she ever wanted and can defeat that demon in her head telling her this is of her own making. She deserves a listening ear and proper therapy to deal with the trauma she endured.*

"Swallowed a whole bottle of pills, with a small bottle of Jack Daniel's, and I STILL WOKE UP!" One disappointed elderly woman grunted, after telling us she was on day nineteen.

I had outgoing peers, some that were mute, and all had been through hell. These people's stories about the circumstances that had brought them to Dillard Manor were sometimes outlandish.

"I cannot use my real name because these places will sometimes rotate you through inpatient mental health to jail and just keep circulating you and abusing you." Another peer confided in me.

I cannot confirm or deny the truth of their stories, as I did not experience them. But I found them a hell of a lot easier to believe after what I endured. I hope that someday these amazing people all have an opportunity to express their stories.

Mental illness is treated shamefully in this country. I did not feel like I was being swept up in love to keep me safe from harm while my brain healed, while I put myself back together. I did not feel cared for.

I did not expect a spa week. However, I did expect that when I needed assistance, for which I was paying exorbitant amounts of money, I would be treated like I paid for that help. I didn't expect to be treated like the facility was somehow doing me a giant favor by allowing me to stay. You work for the patient when you are the doctor or the hospital. That is how business works.

THROUGH ANOTHER'S EYES

Jason Bjorn

The first business that I attended to when I found out that Manda was not being treated appropriately was to call Kriston. Now, for some odd reason, Kriston did not exist. I found out that she worked at some call center for multiple hospitals.

Then I went back to the Google reviews that I had noticed while trying to find emergency assistance for Manda. I found on the negative reviews, which was all of them, that a phone number was posted so that folks could call and address any issues. I called that number. A robot on the phone took my complaint. Another call center and the person I spoke with stated that he would direct my complaint to the correct hospital.

A couple of hours later, Betty (Manda's patient advocate) called me. She wanted to hear my concerns so that they could be confronted. Manda had no idea that she even had a patient advocate. *I would love to define what a care coordinator and a patient advocate entails at Dillard Manor, but I could not honestly tell you. I have no idea.*

I tried to be reasonable. "Look, Betty, is that your name? Manda's medical issues are not being treated or managed as promised. She uses cannabis for the discomfort at home…"

Betty interrupted me. "Cannabis is not allowed at Dillard Manor."

"I understand that. I'm not suggesting that Manda be permitted to use it there, rather informing you that she needs an alternative intervention. Kriston, the woman we originally spoke to via webcam, is evidently no longer involved in Manda's treatment plan, but she made many promises that have not been kept," I snapped back.

"I'm so sorry about that. I..." Betty stammered.

I turned the tables on Betty. "Have you ever seen Manda? Do you even know what she looks like?"

Betty collected herself. "No. But I can assure you that I will visit her as soon as I hang up this phone."

Betty is the woman who Manda had a vague memory of entering her room and thought was from human resources.

On day two, Dr. S. called me. The first that I had heard from him.

"I'm sorry, but I got tied up yesterday, and so could not speak to you." His conversational tone implied disregard of Manda and her plight.

I was livid. "You obviously don't give a damn about your patients! What the hell do you do all day out there at Dillard Manor?"

Dr. S stuttered. I could hear the defeat in his voice as he apologized. I could tell he was overwhelmed.

Even so, he still did not share a treatment plan for Manda with me. He informed me of exactly zero regarding Manda's care, even though Manda's paperwork indicated that I should have access to all treatment plans, actions, and decisions.

I stopped by for visiting hours and took two of our sons with me to visit their mom. Whitney was in the room with Manda. She left the family to visit but whispered to me on the way out, "I will call you in just a bit after you have finished your family time."

During our chat, Dr. S. stated. "Whitney will be giving you a call to discuss Manda's care today."

Whitney never called.

As Whitney left the room, she shut the door, and the boys and I stayed for our forty-five minutes. The nurse then scolded us for closing the door and yelled at our 10-year-old son. I let her have it.

I then demanded to talk to Betty. "She will be out to talk to you in just a moment." The receptionist assured me.

I paced in the lobby for fifteen to twenty minutes to see her, and she never showed up—another lack of responsibility on the part of Dillard Manor.

I did eventually get Betty on the phone. I inquired whether Dillard Manor had gotten a hold of Manda's doctor yet? She was admitted late Monday evening, and this was Wednesday! Betty did not know the answer to that question but specified that she would make sure it happened.

After reading through three hundred pages of medical records, I discovered that at this time, they had still not contacted Manda's primary care physician regarding her health issues.

"Pardon us for not being convinced," I sharply replied.

While attempting to get a hold of Betty, a co-worker of hers answered the phone, and during the brief conversation, she slipped up and said, "Betty is not by position a patient advocate. She works in administration, but we are down an advocate that is on maternity leave."

THAT'S MY LOVE

Through the Years

By the third day, the day of discharge, not one person on the staff had any thought of keeping me past the 72-hour hold.

On my final day at Dillard Manor, Amber, my new care coordinator, took the brunt of our frustration and emotional turmoil. Amber left in tears after Jason and I related to her what had happened, when she saw how frightened and paranoid I was sitting on the bed, visibly trembling and exhausted, evident physical strain, weak from three days without nutrition. My memory of talking to Amber in my room with Jason is foggy. But I do recollect one thing.

With tears in his eyes, Jason pointed to me, looked directly at Amber, and said. "You don't understand. That's my love!"

That was one of those moments that will forever be etched into my heart. Jason's words also gave me a much-needed reality check that I would be safe soon. I didn't feel secure, but I knew that Jason would not let Dillard Manor cause me more trauma. I knew that he was getting me out of there.

(clockwise from top left): 1. ATV riding 2007, not Manda's favorite hobby, but Jason's happy place! 2. Jason and Manda's engagement photo with Manda's family farm barn standing tall in the background, 2006. 3. Romantic, amazing evening after being apart for three weeks, Downtown Denver, Colorado, 2009. The night Manda fell in love with the cucumber melon martini. 4. Jason and Manda at Colorado Rockies game, 2009. 5. "When the bones are good, the rest don't matter." —*The Bones*, Maren Morris

(clockwise from top left): 1. Jason and Manda at Jason's 38th birthday, February 2020. 2. Jason and Manda, 2014. 3. Jason and Manda at their dear friends' wedding, 2013. 4. That's my love!

FLIGHT MODE

On the day of discharge, Dr. S ushered me into an empty meeting room for a quick chat. We had not spent a lot of time together, so I found it odd, not threatening, but strange.

"I'm so sorry that all of this happened to you. This hospitalization could have helped someone like you, but things went wrong. Instead of helping you, we have traumatized you." The look on his face spoke to his remorse.

He then brought up the idea of an Intensive Outpatient Program (IOP). For six weeks, I would come on an outpatient basis to Dillard Manor for group therapy three days a week for three hours each day. The purpose of this would be to overcome what had occurred in Dillard Manor and the issues that had brought me there in the first place.

I felt my flight response kick in, and I would have signed a contract with the devil if that meant that I could stroll out the door of that place and never look back. I also admittedly wanted help. I knew that I was not okay. I was well aware of that. I agreed to meet with the IOP therapist, Liz, while nurses and doctors prepared the discharge paperwork.

I couldn't believe that a therapist like Liz was being hidden in that building. In her calm and warm presence, I felt at ease for a moment. Liz and I went over the details of the treatment and the cost. I knew that this woman did not know me, that she had little idea what had transpired. I do not recall if I was even nice to Liz. I do remember the cost of treatment: $7,500.00.

This is how business is run in the United States of America. One may go in and pay tons of money for inpatient care, which is not received. When care is not received, one would expect any contract signed to be void. But no, one still must pay for care not received. Then one is expected to pay for additional therapy that one requires after the traumatizing experience that one just paid for.

I resigned myself to the inevitable and signed up for six weeks of IOP. In a clearer head in February 2018 I reported their negligence to our insurance provider so that they may dispute charges with Dillard Manor.

Admittedly pissed that Dillard Manor had the audacity to demand that we pay for the IOP. I was still so grateful for the IOP therapist.

The balance of power was off. I was in a state of mind that sought freedom, nothing else. I had been kept in a mental hospital for three days in excruciating pain, fighting for basic kindness. I felt psychologically broken.

I signed the discharge papers, and the nurse knew that Jason would not allow Dillard Manor to keep me past the 72-hour hold, the paperwork I had initially signed. The nurses rushed to discharge me on time. They had had enough of the bombardment of the Jones family for the last three days.

Dillard Manor had me ready for discharge at 5:00 on the dot. The nurse checked the clock as she reviewed my personal belongings with me. Meanwhile Jason paced the waiting room.

After my discharge, I progressed like that proverbial molasses in January. I had more panic attacks than I did before I went into Dillard Manor; I had more significant anxiety. I struggled every single day.

I was not the only person traumatized by that terrifying experience. It took a jumbo toll on Jason. He held our family together while also advocating for me. In addition, he dealt with extreme guilt because he took me to the hospital in the first place. Even though I needed to be hospitalized, I did not in any way deserve to be treated and abused the way that I was.

None of it was Jason's fault. He was doing the best that he could in a crisis.

FEELING ALL THE FEELS

The Intensive Outpatient Program was a six-week group therapy environment where a therapist, Liz, led the group. The most significant number of people in the group at one time for me was seven. In the beginning, there were just two.

Sessions were three days a week for three hours each day. IOP was an experience that I thought I would hate, but I ended up with a sisterhood of validation, love, support, and the knowledge I am not alone.

Folks from all professions and personalities suffer from mental illness. IOP made me realize that I was not crazy because I saw that no one else was crazy. Just overwhelmed, people-pleasers, all of them had endured past trauma. Like me, some of them grappled with physical illness—all human beings fighting to stay afloat in the pressure cooker of life that our society has designed.

Mental illness is a physical illness also. It's your brain! Without a brain, you cease to exist. It is the most crucial organ in the body. It may get sick too. It may become overpowered by external and internal forces as any other organ does. It hurts inside also. As for me, I would get overwhelming pressure in my chest and stomach, my other aliments flared up, and I was unable to regulate my breathing. The whole body is affected when one is stricken with mental illness.

I gained valuable insight into myself through the feedback of others in the program. I found answers to questions that I had been pondering for as long as I could remember. I realized that my walls did not come up because of how tough I was. It was because of the fear of rejection and judgment. I also developed deep remorse for the impatience I had developed with my mother over my life. I felt the strong urge to apologize and let her know I loved her. I felt that I had almost bullied my mom. Mom was the safe place for my frustrations, fear, and rejection, and it was time to repay that with more kindness.

Manda and her mother, 1987

The light; I was making progress. The IOP was an excellent fit for me because of the academic structure; I learn better that way. I acquired several skills that have supported me in setting healthy boundaries, knowing how to communicate during hard conversations, breathing, and meditating.

Most importantly, I forged strong friendships with others from all walks of life who had the same extreme internal turmoil. These friendships further stripped away my tendency to judge anyone else. It convinced me that there would come a time when I am incapable of a judgmental thought at all.

MANDA'S TOOL CHEST

1. Wise Mind ~ **Wise Mind** is the balance between your rational mind and your emotional mind, the happy medium. I was taken by this tool and recall stopping myself and focusing on getting myself into Wise Mind. Below is a visual of what this tool means.

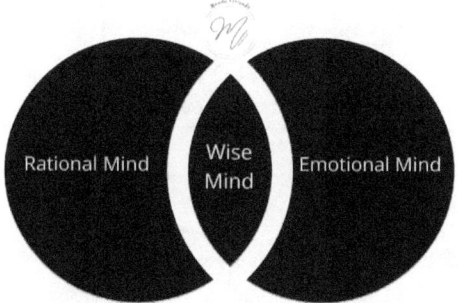

2. Radical Acceptance ~ **Radical Acceptance** was the first tool that I internalized. It taught me that two things might be true at the same time. You may deeply love someone and, at the same time, choose not to interact with that person for your own self-care. You may forgive, yet still walk away.

3. Opposite Action ~ **Opposite Action** is when you feel like a task is too daunting, and you feel anxiety, and instead of sitting down on the couch, you do the opposite and complete the chore, from laundry to spring cleaning.

I had been depressed for years. Doing the laundry had, at times, been a monumental job for me. That may sound nuts if you have never dealt with depression or your experience is different. For me, performing simple tasks became quite difficult during times when anxiety and depression got the best of me.

As a tool, Opposite Action is allowing me to overcome my depression and anxiety in tiny increments.

"I get overwhelmed thinking about a task, and by the end of my thought process, a load of laundry seems equivalent to climbing a mountain!" I said, in class discussion.

"Do one load of laundry and call it a day." Liz enlightened me. So instead of feeling unhinged about doing laundry for hours, I now had the kids bring me what they needed to have washed each night and let them put it in the washing machine. I then did the load before bed. This way, I had taken a bitty step and accomplished something huge at the same time.

4. STOP Skill ~ Picture a stop sign, then imagine that you STOP when you feel like you cannot regulate your emotional self or change your mindset.

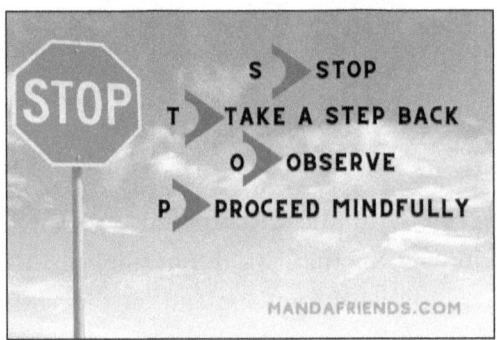

The STOP Skill has been a lifesaver for me! It helps keep me from going down the rabbit hole! When I feel overpowered, hurt, rejected, or any other emotion, I have learned how to STOP, check the facts, and proceed from a calmer state of mind. Sometimes I table specific conversations or tasks and revisit them later.

The other thing about the IOP is that participation brings up every part of yourself that you hide from. I had experiences that I had buried so deep that they were not retrieved until the moment when a peer or Liz spoke a single word. This was not negative, but it was hard to deal with.

Sometimes after sessions, I felt like weights had been lifted from my shoulders, sometimes I felt happy, sometimes I bawled all the way home. A roller coaster ride.

I had a grisly four days before I graduated from the IOP in March 2019. On the last day, you get to have a little celebration with those remaining in the class. I was terrified of leaving that haven with Liz and my friends. I was unable to use any of my tools. My brain was overwhelmed, struggling to process all that was happening in my environment. I had several panic attacks. I scratched my forearms and starved myself (another way of self-harm for me), though since my colitis had worsened over the last four years, I rarely had an appetite.

I had not cut or physically caused injury to myself in four or five years prior, apart from the day I was hospitalized at Dillard Manor. I had not starved myself in five years.

I was honest with the IOP therapist and my peers in the group about the self-harm and my inability to self-regulate, in other words, to keep my emotions in check.

They did not judge me; they embraced me.

Self-harm and a suicide attempt are two different things. When I would self-harm, it was never to kill myself; it was to distract my brain from the anxiety and fears built up inside me. It was to see the blood and feel the burning, feeling my stomach so empty it was painful, a visual and sensory distraction from internal turmoil. To explain better, some turn to alcohol to numb their mind, and I turned to self-harm. Like the mini version above, the toolbox is there to guide me, to help me not to arrive at the point that I would resort to unhealthy coping mechanisms such as self-harm.

It is essential to know and recognize the signs of depression and anxiety to prevent a steep fall into despair. When you recognize it, you could take preventive measures, such as participating in therapy, speaking positive affirmations, working with a life coach, whatever you need to do to care for yourself. It would be best if you accept your mind and body's boundaries, too, as a way of self-care.

I overdid it during those four inglorious days. I ignored the signs that I was not well in my mind. I was not practicing self-care.

In the four days leading to IOP graduation, I know what triggered my short-lived collapse. I overdid it. I did not practice self-care. I ran around like a wild woman from 7:00 in the morning until 9:00 at night. During that time, I did several tasks that overwhelmed me.

I had to run into a Super Mart. I'm not too fond of loud and chaotic environments that have lots of lights. I like small stores, with fewer people, less noise, less bedlam. This time, however, the visit couldn't be avoided.

I then had to talk to the school principal about an incident with a bus driver.

I was parked in front of the grade school waiting for my son to come out of an after-school program when a bus driver punched my passenger side car window where my nine-year-old daughter was sitting! I was pissed, to say the least, he could have knocked that window out on my child! So I was livid. That did not help my emotional state. It happened to all be on camera, so that was a good thing for my complaint. He claimed I was in his way.

The next day my daughter forgot her bookbag.

Then I drove to my ten-year-old son's wrestling practice, where there was lots of noise.

I completed a plethora of errands of this sort. I was never stopping to get in tune with my mind and body.

It had drained me mentally and physically, and with graduation from the IOP looming, my anxiety peaked, and I couldn't regulate my emotional self.

Jason and I identified the problem together. I needed some more help mastering all the work that came with being a mother, wife, entrepreneur, and chronically ill.

Graduation day, March 2019, was hard. Graduation meant that I must move on. It also meant that I no longer had the privilege of meeting Liz, the magnificent therapist, and all fabulous women three times a week anymore. I loved them; we understood each other; we were kind to one another. We built each other up, never kicked down.

Graduation day was filled with tears, gifts from the heart, cards with messages of positivity, love, and hugs. If you knew me personally, you would know that I am not into hugging or much physical contact, but I was on graduation day. It was a simple white room with a big table that could seat around ten adults. What happened in that room was not simple. It was beautiful. I was greeted with gifts from the hearts of theses gorgeous souls that I had endured with, cried with, helped, and accepted help from. I gave them gifts from the heart and cards about what positives I saw in them, the strengths I had witnessed, and their resolve to conquer their demons.

I came home after graduation and was greeted with even more love! My kids and Jason presented me with a card, then we watched movies, talked, and stayed in the NOW.

In the months after graduation, my sister, my sister-in-law, and my closest friends started checking in with me more often. My tanks were no longer empty.

I also understood that boundaries and self-care needed to be prioritized moving forward as I healed, and as my lifestyle changed. Graduation didn't mean that I was fixed. I must now use the tools that I received in my tool chest and recognize when I am slipping and when I need to take a couple of steps back.

One goal that I hope to achieve, which I read aloud to my peers and Liz on graduation day, is to build a Zen garden. Nature is important to me, as are those who I love alive and gone. This garden will have a piece of them and a big part of me.

The earth and music have always been my version of church, and I will have a symbol for each of the wonderful women that I met through the IOP. I will also have a symbol for the beautiful soul who led my group therapy, Liz, who guided us through some trying times and hard topics. I hope that all of these incredible people have it all one day!

REALIZING
THE TRAUMA

I did not see the extent of the trauma that I experienced until two weeks after the IOP graduation. During my second visit to the ER for vomiting blood and severe abdominal and back pain in those two weeks. I had relentless cramps and heavy bleeding from my intestines and my esophagus.

I called my doctor, and the nurses in his office directed me to go to the emergency room closest to me. I always tried to avoid the ER because it is crowded and generally unbearable, but this was the hospital with which my doctor was affiliated. My doctor had written a protocol, in my medical chart, for my colitis flare-ups. This was in hopes of instructing ER doctors what interventions were necessary to stop this and what signs were for hospitalization.

"You are not bleeding from your intestines. I checked for blood." Dr. Comfort *(I did not make that name up!)*

"I can literally show you I am bleeding! What the hell are you talking about!!" I fiercely fought his ridiculous claim.

He couldn't dismiss the blood I was vomiting but decided to lie about my bleeding intestines. I will never understand why. He would do nothing for the pain.

"I am not giving you pain medication. You do not even have colitis." Dr. Comfort argued with me.

"Look at my doctor's notes for these situations, and I was diagnosed with Colitis is 2008, before you were even a doctor!" Low blow?

Maybe. However, his claims seem out of this world and ignorant, especially considering I had undiagnosed C Diff.

The classless and sanctimonious Dr. Comfort drugged me because I lost it. I cried, which escalated the pain substantially. "I can't! You seriously can fuck the fuck off!" I was terrified, and to the point, I was in fight mode. Unusual for people-pleasing Manda!

I felt backed into a corner like I had to fight for my life. That ER ordeal lasted for six hours, all of which came straight out of science fiction!

At my follow up with my primary doctor he said, "I am looking at your records and Dr. Comfort never tested your samples for blood." *Motherfucker!*

The next day, still in so much agony that I couldn't stand up straight, I went back to the hospital sobbing, "I need to speak with who is in charge of the emergency room department."

The front desk ran by volunteers, ushered me to the elevator, pushed the button for me, and told me to speak to Allison. When I arrived at the office, I asked for Allison.

"We will grab her, but ma'am, you do not look well, and we need you in a wheelchair." The receptionist urgently called for the chair. As the chair arrived and the receptionist gently lowered my pain riddled body into the chair, Allison came from the back and immediately started helping her.

"What can I do for you? You look like you need medical attention." Allison stated, perplexed.

Allison, a patient coordinator, called the head emergency room nurse to her office to tell them my story.

It was then that I divulged what had happened to me.

They cried with me. The professionals felt awful and advised me to go to the ER and offered to take me downstairs to the ER and into a direct bed, meaning they would bypass the waiting room and give me a room immediately. I refused. I was too scared.

They pleaded with me to go to another ER in the area, one at which I would feel more comfortable because I was dehydrated and in gut-wrenching pain. I finally agreed to go to the ER at a different hospital. I returned to Colorado General. The emergency room physician at Colorado General did not think that my physical illness was anything other than my typical colitis flare. The difference was that Colorado General understood the pain, nausea, sleep deprivation, vomiting, and terror of my *normal* colitis flare, and the ER doctor treated my symptoms before sending me home.

A few days after the ER visit to Colorado General, I had an appointment with my new gastroenterologist. I had booked this appointment two months before this time, and finally, she performed a simple test and discovered that I had the C. diff infection mentioned above. C. diff is a potentially fatal infection in the colon. It causes inflammation, dehydration, vomiting, and severe abdominal cramping. This explained the punishing abdominal pain and the severe sickness that I had weathered.

Jeez! If only one doctor had listened to me in the five months prior to that.

THE CALM AFTER THE STORM

My family is doing much better now, over a year later. The kids and Jason and I learn to communicate with each other and use the tools that I learned in the IOP to resolve issues for the whole family. I taught the kids to use *I* statements, using statements such as *I feel like my anxiety is heightened.* In lieu of, *you are making my anxiety terrible!*

I have always tried my best to correct my childhood situations and experiences, the parts that aided in the development of my low self-worth and low self-esteem. This stemmed from my father's verbal abuse while under the influence and expectations placed on me that I did not always feel I did or could live up to. I do not call my children names. I do not resent my children; I do not envy them; I do not betray their trust. I genuinely want my children to have a better life than I did as a child. So I try not to repeat the mistakes that hurt me so badly. Through the IOP I learned that even with those cycles of abuse broken, I still had work to do, to not inflict upon my children the same difficulties I encountered in my childhood. My children are my reason to do my best.

My mother-in-law, Sandy, passed away from cancer on April 24, 2019. Her passing was an enormous blow to the entire family. She was the grandma that my kids deserved. She loved them with her whole heart. Her presence is so greatly missed and always will be. She was the rock, the glue, the center of our family. She was an irreplaceable sounding board for me as a mother and a daughter. Our late-night talks will forever be cherished memories for me.

Jason and his mother, Sandy
Dancing at Jason and Manda's wedding January 6, 2007

Jason and I hope that our story sparks a change or serves as a reference for others who must navigate America's mental healthcare system's treacherous waters.

I did obtain the three-hundred pages of medical records generated from my three-day stay at Dillard Manor.

I did not develop anxiety, depression, and emotional regulation issues overnight. It was caused by a combination of childhood traumas, broken family ties, lack of support, self-isolation, self-seclusion, motherhood stresses, life stress in general, and guilt. Processing that kind of trauma and turmoil may take years for some. I am one of those individuals.

The choices that I made in certain areas of my life as a confused and lost youth haunted me. My self-talk, at times, was not just negative; it was mean.

For what my advice is worth, seek help when you see your child slipping. Take a step back and look at the stressors in your child's life.

If you are an addict and a parent, get treatment, and spend the rest of their lives, showing your children that you love and support them unconditionally.

If you are an adult, the ball is in your court. Seek treatment. Be proactive with your mental health care.

If you face a life challenge that seems unmanageable, participate in therapy so that you may acquire the tools necessary to cope and avoid the darker side of your mind.

I have been diagnosed with Major Depressive Disorder, Post-Traumatic Stress Disorder, and Generalized Anxiety Disorder. Writing that on paper is uncomfortable, as the shame starts to seep through, but the tools in my tool chest help guide me when I can't quite see the shore through the thick fog.

Some days I feel like a gorgeous wife and a confident businesswoman. On other days I feel like an exhausted, over-extended mother of four who must fight to get out of bed. Every day is different, but every day is worth it.

AFTERWORD

It is September 2020, and it's been more than a year since my historic and illustrious breakdown. I have a new psychiatrist and have finally found the right medication for me, Lamictal.

This is not an advertisement or an endorsement for Lamictal. Simply put, after years of hunting for the right medication and now finding something that makes me feel like me is quite liberating. I'm starting to feel like the girl I used to be, the one who could set her mind to anything and fight until she gets it right.

My physical health challenges remain an uphill climb, and I have no choice but to trudge up those mountains before me. Even still, I can cope most of the time. However, sometimes it is not easy. Here's a picture of me climbing a physical mountain three weeks after back surgery. The Manda of two years ago would not have even attempted!

Proof! Arapahoe National Forest, hiking a mountain with my three sons and husband, three weeks post-op back surgery. June 2020

I find myself searching those overlapping circles in my mind, the rational and the emotional, to find the happy medium before words come out of my mouth or action is taken. I also advocate for myself much better than I did before or humble myself to seek help.

We are making the necessary changes to live a more simple and peaceful life and give our children room to grow. I am learning to ask for help as a mother when I need it. No one can do it all alone and stay sane.

My Zen garden is on hold right now, but I have drawn up plans for how it will look. I have put great thought into what will go into this hallowed place; sunflowers in memory of my mother-in-law Sandy, yellow roses for my marriage, and lilac bushes for my grandfather. I will select special stones for my IOP peers and therapist and engraved stones for those close to me whom I have lost, to remind me to live for them.

I have enormous dreams for this peaceful, yoga-friendly garden. I also have colossal plans for my future because I have a pretty amazing one to look forward to.

As I prepare to publish this book, it is hard not to mention the civil unrest, political divides, massive unemployment, a Global Pandemic COVID19, and an entirely new way of living life. My psychiatrist said to me, "Stay at home does not me, self-isolation." A reminder to still engage. However, I can with the people who give me strength and make me feel at ease. Even if it is from a distance.

Mental healthcare is going to need essential funding and overall changes to take on the task of healing a nation during and after this storm. They are also going to need us to rally, support, fight for, and hold them up during what may prove to be the hardest job of their lives.

From my heart to yours,
Manda

Manda and Jason have opened their blog up to those
who wish to speak their truth. No cost. Please visit
Mandafriends.com/blog
and contact us to discuss telling yours.
What's your story?

TESTIMONIALS

At a dark time in my life, IOP was my one safe place. I could be broken and honest, without fearing judgement or consequence, and I was welcomed into a beautiful community of strong and inspiring women, who all held each other up with love and wisdom. It was a powerfully healing experience. ~ Monica Buettel, Ph.D.

IOP saved my life. It showed me the beauty of the human spirit. IOP introduced me to some of the strongest women I have ever met. Though we came from so many different backgrounds, ages, and places in our lives, we became a family. And I don't think that I would be here today without the bond that I made with those amazing women. ~ Haley, College Student

R.C. is a talented and beautiful young woman. For a few weeks during the IOP, it was just the two of us, and we got to be quite close. I felt much like a big sister to her and was so taken by her talent. During class she would, with just pen and paper, create masterpieces. She drew this for me as a graduation present. She knew I had a love for Orca's and I have never possessed a more precious piece of art. ~ Manda Jones

Orca by R.C.

www.ingramcontent.com/pod-product-compliance
Lightning Source LLC
Chambersburg PA
CBHW021959290426
44108CB00012B/1129